JIMMY BUTLER

NBA STAR

By Douglas Lynne

Book design by Christine Ha
Cover design by Jake Nordby

Photographs ©: Lynne Sladky/AP Images, cover, 1; Chris Szagola/AP Images, 4, 7, 8; Shutterstock Images, 10; Morry Gash/AP Images, 13; Darren Hauck/AP Images, 14; Nam Y. Huh/AP Images, 16; Chris Williams/Icon Sportswire/AP Images, 19, 23; Nick Wass/AP Images, 20; Red Line Editorial, 22

Press Box Books, an imprint of Press Room Editions.

Library of Congress Control Number: 2020901608

ISBN
978-1-63494-218-8 (library bound)
978-1-63494-236-2 (paperback)
978-1-63494-254-6 (epub)
978-1-63494-272-0 (hosted ebook)

Distributed by North Star Editions, Inc.
2297 Waters Drive
Mendota Heights, MN 55120
www.northstareditions.com

Printed in the United States of America
082020

ABOUT THE AUTHOR

Douglas Lynne is a freelance writer. He spent many years working in the media, first in newspapers and later for online organizations, covering everything from breaking news to politics to entertainment to sports. He lives in Minneapolis, Minnesota.

TABLE OF CONTENTS

1

IN RARE AIR

On most nights, Jimmy Butler played an important role for the Chicago Bulls. But on January 14, 2016, the team needed him to really step up. Former league Most Valuable Player (MVP) Derrick Rose was out that night. So was star center Pau Gasol. Butler was a good player. But he was not used to carrying a team.

However, Butler took over that night against the Philadelphia 76ers. He led all

Jimmy Butler drives to the hoop during his big game against the 76ers.

scorers with 12 points in the first quarter. He added 13 more in the second quarter. It was the start of a special night.

Butler was already known around the National Basketball Association (NBA) as a great defensive player. But that night, he showed he could put points on the board, too. He was scoring from everywhere.

FROM THE STRIPE

Butler racked up a lot of his points from the free-throw line against the Sixers. He made 21 of 25 free throws he attempted. The rest of the Bulls shot six free throws all game.

Butler also was dishing out assists to his teammates. He assisted on or scored almost every Chicago basket in the fourth quarter. And he was grabbing rebounds, too.

Butler led a comeback after the Bulls had let a 16-point lead slip away.

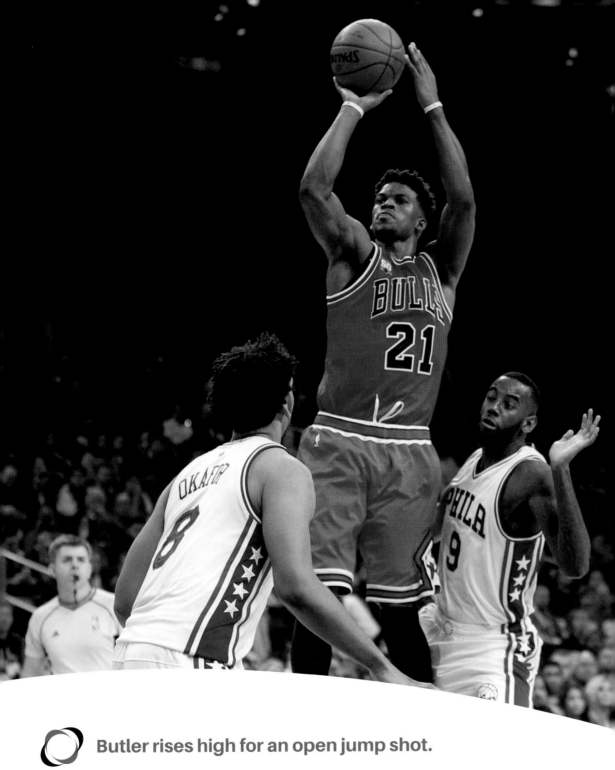

Butler rises high for an open jump shot.

The Bulls had lots of success when the ball was in Butler's hands.

Butler scored his 51st point with less than two minutes to go. That made him the first Chicago Bull to score 50 points in one game in 12 years. The game went to overtime. In the extra period, Butler added two more points to give Chicago a 113-108 lead. That was all the points they needed as they won 115-111.

Butler finished with 53 points, 10 rebounds, and six assists. The last Bull to match those totals in one game was Michael Jordan. Butler wasn't on Jordan's level. But there was no doubt he could be the Bulls' next big star. However, it didn't work out exactly like that.

JIMMY BUTLER, MOST POINTS IN A GAME
THROUGH 2019-20 SEASON

- **53** at Philadelphia, January 14, 2016
- **52** vs. Charlotte, January 2, 2017
- **43** vs. Detroit, December 18, 2015
- **42** at Toronto, January 3, 2016
- **42** vs. Toronto, January 7, 2017

2

TOUGH CHILDHOOD

Jimmy Butler was homeless when he was 13 years old. After many conflicts with his mother, she kicked him out of the house.

"I don't like the look of you," Jimmy remembered his mom saying. "You gotta go."

Jimmy couldn't turn to his dad, who had abandoned the family shortly after Jimmy was born in 1989. So Jimmy

Jimmy grew up in a suburb of Houston, Texas.

reached out to friends. He would live with a family for a few weeks at a time. Then it was time to move on and find a new home.

Jimmy grew up in a suburb of Houston, Texas, called Tomball. Basketball was one thing Jimmy could turn to. He was the best player on his high school team. He hoped basketball would help him get to college. It ended up finding him a home.

TEXAS LEGEND

Jimmy Butler remains a legend in his hometown. The fans there were proud of him for making it to the NBA. In 2017, 10 years after he graduated from Tomball High School, the school retired his No. 1 jersey. No Tomball player would ever wear it again.

Jimmy was shooting baskets one summer day before his senior year. A freshman named Jordan Leslie challenged him to a three-point shooting contest. The two instantly became friends.

Jimmy eventually ended up in Milwaukee, Wisconsin, playing for Marquette University.

Jimmy showed NBA scouts that he was ready to play at the next level.

They became so close that Jordan's family offered Jimmy a place to live. They already had seven kids in the house. But Jimmy fit right in.

Jimmy averaged nearly 20 points per game as a senior in high school. His teammates voted him MVP. But only a few colleges were interested in him. Jimmy instead decided to attend Tyler Junior College in Tyler, Texas.

Jimmy played well that year and got the attention of Marquette University. The Golden Eagles offered him a scholarship. Jimmy had to earn playing time at first. He went from starting no games as a sophomore to full-time starter as a junior and senior.

NBA teams started to take notice. Jimmy waited to see where the 2011 draft would take him.

3

TRAVELING STAR

Jimmy Butler was a first-round draft pick. But just barely. The Chicago Bulls took him 30th overall. Many players taken that low don't play big roles in the NBA. That was the case for Butler early on. But he started to play more minutes his second season. He even started all 12 Bulls playoff games that year.

Butler showed that he could be a star player, especially on defense. By his third

Butler (21) had a rough transition to the NBA as a rookie.

season, Butler was a full-time starter. The Bulls counted on him as part of their team. But he still had to improve on offense.

Butler took a big step forward in 2014–15. He developed a more accurate jump shot and averaged 20 points per game. Suddenly he was a leader on both offense and defense. He was rewarded with a spot in the All-Star Game. And the Bulls rewarded him with a new contract.

GOOD AS GOLD

Butler made his international debut in the summer of 2016. He played with Team USA at the 2016 Summer Olympics. Butler played in all eight games as Team USA won the gold medal.

Chicago traded star guard Derrick Rose before the 2016–17 season. That left Butler as the team's best player. Losing the former MVP hurt, but Butler led the Bulls to a playoff spot. They nearly pulled off an upset over the Boston Celtics but lost in six games.

Butler played for Team USA in the 2016 Rio Olympics.

The Heat became Butler's fourth team in four years when he was traded in 2019.

The Bulls decided to make big changes after the season. They traded Butler to the Minnesota Timberwolves. He led the Wolves to the playoffs for the first time in 14 seasons. But early in the next season, he was traded again, this time to Philadelphia.

Butler often clashed with teammates in both Minnesota and Philadelphia. He set high standards for the other players. That sometimes caused problems. He was traded yet again to Miami before the 2019-20 season.

Butler got a fresh start in Miami. He averaged 20 points per game for the fifth time in six years. He also set new career highs in rebounds and assists per game. Butler was playing like the star he knew he could be. And with his new team, Butler set his sights on trying to win his first NBA title.

TIMELINE MAP

1. **Houston, Texas: 1989**
   Jimmy Butler is born on September 14.

2. **Tomball, Texas: 2007**
   Butler graduates from Tomball High School.

3. **Tyler, Texas: 2008**
   Butler enrolls and plays one season at Tyler Junior College.

4. **Milwaukee, Wisconsin: 2008**
   Butler receives a scholarship offer from Marquette University and goes on to a three-year college career.

5. **Newark, New Jersey: 2011**
   The Chicago Bulls select Butler with the 30th pick in the NBA Draft on June 23.

6. **Chicago, Illinois: 2012**
   Butler makes his NBA debut on January 1, scoring two points in a win over the Memphis Grizzlies.

7. **Philadelphia, Pennsylvania: 2016**
   Butler scores a career-high 53 points in an overtime win over the 76ers on January 14.

8. **Miami, Florida: 2019**
   Butler signs with the Miami Heat on July 6 following a trade.

AT-A-GLANCE

JIMMY BUTLER

Birth date: September 14, 1989

Birthplace: Houston, Texas

Position: Shooting guard/small forward

Height: 6 feet 7 inches

Weight: 230 pounds

Current team: Miami Heat (2019–)

Past teams: Marquette Golden Eagles (2008–11), Chicago Bulls (2011–17), Minnesota Timberwolves (2017–18), Philadelphia 76ers (2018–19)

Major awards: NBA All-Star (2015, 2016, 2017, 2018, 2020), NBA Most Improved Player (2015), Olympic gold medalist (2016)

Accurate through the 2019–20 season.

MORE INFORMATION

To learn more about Jimmy Butler, go to **pressboxbooks.com/AllAccess**.

These links are routinely monitored and updated to provide the most current information available.

GLOSSARY

assists
Passes that lead to made shots in basketball.

draft
A system by which sports leagues divide up new talent.

freshman
A first-year student.

junior college
A two-year college that often includes athletic programs.

scholarship
Money given to a student to cover college expenses, often in exchange for playing sports.

upset
When one team unexpectedly beats another.

INDEX